DATE DUE

MR 6'98			
MY 13'98			
MY 26'98			
DE 18'98			
MR 2 '99			
JE 10 02			
DE 21 02			

DEMCO 38-296

For all the families, for mine and yours, and for the families of the fields.

EARTH ANGELS
MIGRANT CHILDREN IN AMERICA

NANCY BUIRSKI

INTRODUCTION BY
Henry G. Cisneros

AFTERWORD BY
Rubén Blades

POMEGRANATE ARTBOOKS, SAN FRANCISCO, CALIFORNA

A CHAMELEON BOOK

© 1994 Nancy Buirski
© 1994 Introduction by Henry G. Cisneros
© 1994 Afterword by Rubén Blades
© 1994 Compilation Chameleon Books, Inc.

Published by Pomegranate Artbooks
Box 6099, Rohnert Park, California 94927

Produced by Chameleon Books, Inc.
211 West 20th Street, New York, New York 10011

Extracts from THE GRAPES OF WRATH by John Steinbeck
Copyright 1939, renewed © 1967 by John Steinbeck
Used by permission of Viking Penguin, a division of
Penguin Books USA Inc.

SOMETHING IN THE RAIN © 1994 Trish Hinojosa

Creative director / designer: Arnold Skolnick
Composition: Larry Lorber, Ultracomp
Printer: Oceanic Graphic Printing, Hong Kong

Library of Congress Cataloging-in-Publication Data

Buirski, Nancy.
    Earth angels : migrant children in America / Nancy Buirski.
        p.   cm.
    "A Chameleon book."
    ISBN 0-87654-073-6 : $35.00. – ISBN 0-87654-074-4 (pbk.) : $24.95
1. Children of migrant laborers – United States – Social conditions.
2. Children of migrant laborers – United States – Pictorial works.
3. Migrant agricultural laborers – United States – Social conditions.
4. Migrant agricultural laborers – United States – Pictorial works.
I. Title.
HQ792.U5B85   1994
305.23'08'624 – dc20
                                                    94-12756
                                                      CIP

ACKNOWLEDGMENTS

In any project where great distances are covered one is dependent on the help of many friends and many strangers. Because this book could not have been completed without their assistance, I will try to acknowledge them all. If I have, by chance, left out any individuals, please accept my apologies, and know that this book pays tribute not only to the unsung heroes who work the fields so that we may eat the fruits and vegetables of their labors, but also to this project's contributors, acknowledged or not. There are so many who support and service the migrant families who deserve recognition. Their involvement in my project is but another reflection of their selfless dedication to these workers.

First and foremost, this book would not exist in its final form without the tireless assistance of Román Cruz of Texas, an outreach worker who as a child worked in the fields. One could not ask for a better helpmate; his intelligence, patience and enthusiasm were unmatched. Many of the interviews resulted from Román's persistence and enrich the photographs exponentially.

Thomas Burke, the publisher of Pomegranate Artbooks, saw the value of this project from the beginning. Dedicated to making this a legacy, he encouraged me to go at it without restraint. This book is the product of his uncategorical belief and support. And the final manifestation of the past four years was shaped with the consummate visual skills and sensitivity of Arnold Skolnick. His understanding of the power of image and design has inspired me for the past twenty years of my life. My personal artistic achievements, as well as the ultimate presentation of this project, would not be so without his genius.

Jeffrey Newman of the National Child Labor Committee and his daughter, Andrea Newman, were energetic supporters from the beginning of this venture. The imprimatur of this dedicated committee not only opened doors for me, but extended my responsibility as well. Since the turn of the century, N.C.L.C.'s mission has been and continues to be the safeguarding of children as their lives intersect with the workplace. I am honored to be in the company of Lewis W. Hine, who at the behest of N.C.L.C., made legendary images of children in factories and fields, photographs that continue to symbolize our mandate.

No sooner had Mary Frost received a prestigious N.C.L.C. Lewis Hine Special Service Award for her astounding fund-raising efforts in Olympia, Washington, than she embraced this documentation by raising funds for its survival. She has continued to be an inspiration throughout.

For their assistance in New York State: Jim Schmidt of Farmworker Legal Services; Robert McConnell, M.D., Occupational Medicine at Mt. Sinai Hospital in Manhattan; Chris Pearson, photographic assistant.

Plainview, Texas: William Beardall, Texas Rural Legal Aid; Kay Maris, Plainview Rural Legal Aid; Darryl Thomas, photographic assistant; Trini Gomez and Jesus Moya; outreach workers; Darryl Kremec, U.S. Department of Labor; Martin Tune, grower.

Homestead, Florida: Lisa Levine, South Dade Immigration Association; Connie Berry, educator; Ann Marie Elefthery, Health Access Planner; Peggy Nolan, photographic assistant.

Washington State: Carlos Treviño, Migrant Child Institute; Carlos Diaz, Executive Director, Washington State Migrant Council; Raoul De La Rosa, Office of the Superintendant of Public Instruction; Raoul Arambul, Washington State Migrant Council; Victoria Morales, Washington State Migrant Council; Daria Miller, Washington State Migrant Council; Kristy Cook, photographic assistant.

California: Gloria Naranjo, California Rural Legal Assistance; Benito Sanchez, migrant advocate; Thomas Brill, California Rural Legal Assistance.

The following friends and colleagues whose inspiration—intellectual, visual and spiritual—contributed in unestimable ways: at The New York Times—Kathy Ryan, who nurtured this project from the beginning; Geraldine Shanahan, who helped shape the text; Mark Bussell, Stephen Crowley, Leslie Goldman, Paul Hosefros, Nancy Lee, Michael Kaufman, David Scull and Joe Treaster, as well as many other supportive reporters, editors and photographers; Also Robert Boorstin, Jennifer Coley, Holly Ornstein Carter, Pete Daniel, Lee Daniels, Marco De Plano, Karin Epstein, Rosemary Erph, Donna Ferrato, Abigail Heyman, Nancy Kropp Galdy, Thomas Galdy, Vicki Goldberg, Pamela Hollie Kluge, P.F. Kluge, Arthur Laszlo, David Li, Stan Lichens, Larry Lorber, Jim Mairs, Roberta Marini, Michael Marks, Cathy Michaelson, David Moynehan, Haig Nalbantian, Marina Pastor, Raphael Pastor, Marcy Posner, Fred Ritchin, Kevin Ryan, Lynn Schumann, Martin Scorsese, Jillian Slonim, Charles Treves, Vivian Treves, Burk Uzzle, William Walton, Marc Weiss, George Whittaker and Valerie Wilke.

Nancy Buirski

"and none can care, beyond that room; and none can be cared for, by any beyond that room: and it is a small wonder they are drawn together so cowardly close."

James Agee
"Let Us Now Praise Famous Men," 1939

IN the spare and tedious life of the tenant farmer, James Agee and Walker Evans found a dignity that bordered on the poetic. These people had traveled through the valley of despair and back, returning only with the knowledge that they had each other, even as they abandoned their dreams of a better life. Through years of adversity, made even more acute by the Depression, these sharecroppers sustained themselves through the comfort of the family bond and the value of their work, no matter how meager the financial rewards. Thus, they were praised.

Sadly, little has changed; today's migrant families inherit this mean life and, as if instructed by their figurative ancestors (they are now mostly Mexican-Americans), they have also accepted the mantle of pride in their highly skilled labor. The fact of their movement—like nomads they follow the crop—intensifies their bond. The constant dislocation precludes any real connection to the society around them. This moving family has only itself as an anchor, creating a tightly knit, but otherwise vulnerable community.

The migrant family is one of the last remaining manifestations of families working as an economic unit in this country, a vestige of an earlier time, when families, particularly agrarian, worked as one entity, with each member working towards a common goal. In these families, when children work, it is not a rite of passage, but an economic necessity, essential to the success of the family venture.

It is these working children whom I have found myself drawn to as I photographed migrant families these past four years. They are so affected by the adversities of migrant life, yet they maintain a spirit that transcends their difficult childhood. The adversity is real: migrant farmworkers have the lowest earning power of all occupational groups in the United States, disease is rampant and living conditions are squalid. And the children are hardest hit. If they are in school at all, they must leave it when a harvest is complete, and try to resume studies and social growth wherever they go. In some cases, older children start work in the fields as early as 5 A.M. and attend high school in the early evening. In spite of child labor laws, children as young as four work beside their parents, as their hands are more nimble for picking and their backs more supple for bending. They breathe in pesticides daily, helping to ensure that their life expectancy will probably not exceed 49 years.

What is it like to get an education on the run, making a playground of tractors and pick-up trucks? I have tried to find the child within this incredibly demanding environment, to photograph that spirit. Trips to Texas, upstate New York, Washington State, Florida and California have introduced me to the cultural richness of these people and the heroics of their children. Despite the imposition of serious adult responsibilities, these children do not seem burdened. Nurtured by the tempered strength of a family of survivors, somehow the child inside the working child has been kept alive.

What are the lessons here? At the same time that we mourn the tragedy of so many fractured inner-city families, these migrant youths are finding strength in their place in the family and through their work in the fields. Their own poverty is not to be romanticized, but their tradition explored. How has their culture, the fact of their labor, and the value system of the migrant Mexican-American allowed such a spirit to emerge?

What stimulates the values that are so much at work here? What seems clear from the onset, is that these migrant children, unlike the brutalized, cynical children of our cities' ghettos, are not abandoned. Yes, there are obvious and serious deprivations, but they work beside their parents, defining themselves in the context of their work and their place in the home. Even those who do not physically labor in the fields, but travel nonetheless with the harvest, obtain their identity through the family migration and enterprise. They are moved by the love and hope of a family working together to create a future.

My hope is that these photographs document these children's passage from despair to hope, that they honor these values that work so well now, as they have in all time.

Nancy Buirski

INTRODUCTION

by Henry G. Cisneros

IN 1967 Robert Coles, the well-known child psychologist and political activist, wrote about the "psychological pressures of growing up in the cycle of migrant farmwork." He said, "How literally extraordinary, and in fact how extraordinarily cruel, their lives are: the constant mobility, the leave-takings and the fearful arrivals, the demanding work they often manage to do, the extreme hardship that goes with a meager (at best) income, the need always to gird oneself for the next slur, the next sharp rebuke, except, naturally, for the work that has to be done in the fields. There is...the misery; and it cannot be denied its importance, because not only bodies but minds suffer out of hunger and untreated illness." Nearly three decades later, these same problems and challenges remain: a 1993 study reported that migrant farmworker life still consists mainly of "poverty, hard manual labor, unsanitary living conditions, lack of medical insurance or access to care facilities, high rates of illness, early death, economic uncertainty, and personal humiliation."[1]

I have often walked through migrant labor camps in Texas, California, Florida, and other states, witnessing with my own eyes the poor facilities that house migrant farmworker families and their children, and I ask myself: how can we allow people to live that way in today's America? It particularly pains me to see the suffering of migrant farmworker children, and the expressions of hopelessness in the faces of their parents. I doubt that anyone can visit migrant farmworker families without having their difficult living conditions make an indelible impression on her or his mind. To those who have not seen this world firsthand, there is no better place to start than with this new book of remarkable photographs by Nancy Buirski.

Nancy Buirski, an accomplished photojournalist, has traveled the length and breadth of this country with her camera and her compassion for the people she photographs, following migrant farmworker camps from New York and Florida in the East, California and Washington in the West, and my home state of Texas right in the middle. These pictures tell a complex and revealing story, reminiscent of photographer Dorothea Lange's compelling portraits of migrant farmworkers during the Great Depression in the 1930s, which served as a powerful visual companion to John Steinbeck's classic novel, *The Grapes of Wrath.*

The photos in the following pages both reflect and call forth a wide range of emotions. For example, one can feel a sense of deep anger and injustice at seeing the squalid housing conditions in a California migrant camp ironically named La Palacio, meaning The Palace. Yet along with the sorrow and the sadness, the sun-hardened faces of adults looking old before their time, the children lost in a world of deprivation and constant change, there are also the looks of joy and mischief, hope and dreams, and most of all, the love of brothers and sisters and parents and families, of relatives and friends who defend and protect each other in an unfriendly environment. We can cry for the 29 year-old mother who looks 50, for the children sleeping on the ground because their parents cannot afford even the worst housing, for the babies with not enough to eat; and we can also smile at the children playing games together, taking care of pet animals, and delight at the picture of the "burger queen" with her bright gold paper crown.

Earth Angels should serve as a constant reminder of both the hardships and the triumphs of migrant farmworker children, youngsters who grow up facing a constant cycle of poverty due to the nature of their parents' work. Migrant farmworkers are all too invisible in our society, and yet, they and their children put food on our tables every day. Over one million migrant farmworker children travel through all 50 states and the Commonwealth of Puerto Rico and, with their parents, harvest the fruits and vegetables which we buy in our supermarkets. Occasionally some person or event breaks through the wall of silence to remind us of their plight. In the 1960s and 70s Cesar Chavez, Dolores Huerta, and many other brave farmworkers led hunger strikes, grape and lettuce boycotts, demonstrations and labor strikes to organize the United Farmworkers Union of America, AFL-CIO. A few courageous political leaders like Senator Robert F. Kennedy spoke out about their plight and urged public support, and at time this awareness filtered through the media blockade to reach a wider audience, with several notable examples like the television documentary "Harvest of Shame."

My many years of working with the Texas Migrant Council as Mayor of San Antonio has kept alive my continuing concern for the plight of migrant farmworker families. This awareness has prompted me as Secretary of the U.S. Department of Housing and Urban Development (HUD) to appoint a staffperson (for the first time in the Department's history) to address the migrant farmworker housing needs in this country. Recognizing the importance and the necessity of decent homes, HUD intends to implement a new initiative that will strive to provide decent homes for migrant farmworkers and their children.

I am convinced that it will require interagency cooperation and collaboration amongst pertinent Federal agencies to adequately address the problems of migrant farmworker families. As the National Advisory Council on Migrant Health acknowledges, "The Farmers Home Administration, Department of Housing and Urban Development, Department of Agriculture, and Department of Health and Human Services are in a position to significantly impact the migrant worker housing situation. If they coordinate their efforts and resources we may draw nearer to the time when safe and adequate housing will be available for our migrant workforce. Meanwhile, the migrant farmworker housing situation is caught in a downward spiral."[2]

Migrant farmworker children, like all other children, need safe, decent places to play and enjoy their childhoods. In addition to decent, affordable housing and access to health care, appropriate daycare, pre-school and educational services are essential ingredients for helping migrant farmworker children beat the odds. Many adult migrant farmworkers lack formal schooling, particularly in the English language. Furthermore, "migrant farmworker children are often labeled 'slow learners'" because their education is disrupted by their frequent moves.[3] All of us recognize that in order for migrant farmworker children to learn effectively, they need quiet places in their homes where they can study and do their homework.

Due to the high risk of pesticide exposure and accidents, and "[t]he circumstances of the migrant lifestyle—overcrowding, lack of sanitary living facilities or recreation, and lack of dignity—" migrant farmworker families suffer from numerous health problems. Recent scientific and medical research studies have documented that "farmwork is now the most dangerous occupation in this country, more dangerous even than mining and construction. Although agricultural workers account for only 3 percent of the workforce, they account for 14 percent of work-related deaths."[4]

A comprehensive analysis conducted in 1991 by the U.S. Department of Health and Human Services found that "the disease patterns of . . . [the migrant farmworker] population today are similar to those found in the general population of the U.S. well over sixty years ago. They have high rates of parasitic and infectious diseases including food and water-borne disorders, as well as chronic diseases. The rate of diabetes is as much as 300 percent higher than that of the general population. Migrant farmworkers and their families are more likely to experience significant maternal and newborn health problems, such as high risk pregnancy, as well as hypertension, infectious and dermatological diseases."[5] The life expectancy of migrant farmworkers is estimated to be 49 years, compared to the U.S. national average of 73 years. Infant mortality among California's migrant farmworkers is 30 out of 1,000, more than double the infant mortality rate for the overall U. S. population. Astonishingly, the same study of California farmworkers found the mortality rate among young children more than 50 percent higher than the already high rate for infants.[6]

I have always been inspired by great poetry, and one of my favorites is a poem about the tragic health problems of farmworkers due to their overexposure to chemical pesticides sprayed on the crops they harvest and the fields they work at for so many hours of the day and week. The poem, "Something in the Rain" by Trish Hinojosa, refers to the pesticide spray that permeates the atmosphere around farmworkers' lives, and offers a child's perspective of the fearful experience on poor health, disease, and death:

SOMETHING IN THE RAIN by Trish Hinojosa

Mom and Dad have worked in the fields
I don't know how many years
I'm just a boy but I know how
I go to school when work is slow.

We have seen our country's roads
Bakersfield to Illinois
But when troubles come our way
Oh yes, I've seen my Daddy pray.

There's something wrong with little sister
I hear her crying by my side
Mama's shaking as she holds her
I try to hold them through the night.

There must be something in the rain
I don't know just what that means
"Aguelita" talks of sins of man
and dust that's in our hands.
There must be something in the rain
what else could cause this pain
Airplanes cure those plants so things can grow
I guess there's something in the rain.

Now little sister's gone away
Mama is working hard all day
And me – I guess I understand
About our life – about our land
talkers talk and dreamers dream.
We must find a place between.

Cause there's something in the rain
And there's more here in our hands
"Aguelita's" right about those sins of man
Whose profits rape the land.
And those rains keep pouring down
from the growers to the town and
until we break that killing chain
there's something in the rain.

Let us draw inspiration from these photographs and the moving experience of the lives of migrant farmworker families and children that *Earth Angels* conveys. Together we can break the chain of "something in the rain", and bring prosperity and a better life to all of God's children, young and old, whatever their background, wherever they live and work.

Notes

1. U. S. Dept. of Health and Human Services, National Advisory Council on Migrant Health, Bureau of Primary Health Care, *1993 Recommendations of the National Advisory Council on Migrant Health,* May 1993, pp. 25, 35.

2. *Ibid.* p. 13.

3. *Ibid.* p. 28, see also p. 36.

4. Ingersoll, B., "Farming is Dangerous, but Fatalistic Farmers Oppose Safety Laws," *The Wall Street Journal,* July 20, 1989, p. 1.

5. Marilyn H. Gaston, M. D., Assistant Surgeon General, Director, Bureau of Primary Health Care, Health Resources ad Services Administration, U. S. Department of Health and Human Services, "Testimony to the Commission on Security and Cooperation in Europe," October 9, 1992, in Commission on Security and Cooperation in Europe, *Implementation of the Helsinki Accords: Migrant Farmworkers in the United States* (Washington, D. C., May 1993), p. 240.

6. U. S. Department of Health and Human Services, *1993 Recommendations of the National Advisory Council on Migrant Health,* p. 36.

FARMWORKER SUPPORT PROGRAMS

By Jeffrey F. Newman

Though the plight of the migrant farmworker continues to stand out as a stain on the American landscape, there do exist important national and community-based organizations that provide much-needed support and advocacy services. Because of the nature of migrancy—the endemic poverty, the chronic health problems, the transiency and the resulting lack of political clout—these organizations play an even more critical role on behalf of their constituencies than might be expected. Often they are the one and only voice for groups of farmworkers; the only advocate with educators, health providers, political leaders.

Most of these organizations operate with the leanest kind of budgets, yet the services that they must provide are extensive and constant. They range from national groups like the Farm Labor Organizing Committee (FLOC) and United Farmworkers (UFW) to the National Council of LaRaza (NCLR), the Association of Farmworker Opportunity Programs (AFOP) and the National Child Labor Committee (NCLC) on the national side to local organizations such as various chapters of Rural Opportunities, Inc. (ROI) and hundreds of small but effective community-based groups. Some are advocates, some are service providers and advocates, but all organizations that represent and work on behalf of farmworkers share one thing in common beyond the need for public support: they believe that the farmworker is, despite the current reality, just as entitled to the fulfillment of the American dream as anyone.

Jeffrey F. Newman is the President/Executive Director of the private, non-profit National Child Labor Committee.

"*We plant the cabbage, then clean the cucumber, clean the cabbage, then pick the cukes. Then we start the apples.*"

Israel Gonzales

Esther Gonzales, 15, harvesting cucumbers, Brockport, N.Y.

"My father was born in McAllen, Texas, and my mom was born in Saltillo, Coahuila. But we were raised in McAllen, Michigan, California and Houston. We were also migrants.

"I have twelve children.

"Since '85 we have been going to New York. We usually leave Texas about June 10. We come back about December 12. What I like about New York is that we work for the same farmer all the time that we are up there. When we would migrate to Idaho we would work about three weeks with one farmer then look elsewhere. We would spend our summer in search of work.

"About April they give us a call to find out if we will return and if we plan to take extra family. The main reason I like New York is because the girls go to night school."

Israel Gonzales

Gonzales family arriving for the harvest in the early morning.

Rachel Gonzales, 15.

Nancy Gonzales, 15, Rachel's sister-in-law.

Lidia Gonzales with her daughters, Amelia, 11, Esther, 15, and Beatrice, 18.

Rachel Gonzales eats a cucumber on a break. The field had been sprayed with pesticide the previous day.

"We have to get it all done."
Esther Gonzales

Esther Gonzales finishing the harvest.

Amelia rests after her shower.

Lidia flours the tortillas.

Amelia's sister helps her get ready to go to the mall.

Israel, their father, and Lidia preparing tortillas for the next day's work.

The labor camp, Murton, New York

TEXAS PANHANDLE

"Going and coming and going and coming. To make a living for my family. Now that the children are able to help me, we have gone to Floydada.

"I have my old truck. A '64, which is what takes us and brings us. Our hardship is that sometimes we don't even have good tires. We don't go to make lots of money. We save a little for the children. I am disabled from my back, but I still have to take them. What else can I do?

"We go to work so early in the morning, it is still dark out. My wife is fixing food at 4 A.M., sometimes at 3. I would tell her, why don't you wait a bit. Sometimes in the fields she would be falling asleep. And the kids are in the same boat. But what can you do? If you go in at 8 A.M., you won't be able to work because of the hot sun. That's why we have to take advantage of the cool early mornings. We really don't have a way out of this."

Jorge Zavala

The Zavala family, Estella, 37, Susy, 12, Kristy, 9, and Jorge, 43, leave the Floydada labor camp at 4:30 in the morning for the cotton fields.

Kristy Zavala hoeing cotton with the sun barely up.

Susy Zavala with her hoe.

The Zavala family works in 100 degrees, heavily dressed to protect them from bugs.

Susy, Kristy, and Henry, 15, returning from the fields with their parents.

"Kristy is good in school, but she likes working in the fields too."

"If the farmers say it's O.K. for them to work, it's O.K. We work a little more faster and they like it."
Estella Zavala

"I don't want my children to end up having to do this type of work. But for now I don't have the ability to do anything else. I never had schooling because from a very young age I had to work."
Jorge Zavala

Kristy Zavala at the labor camp with her pet starlings.

Kristy and Susy play with one of the few toys they brought with them from Santa Maria, Texas, 800 miles away.

The family showers as soon as they return from the field. Susy fixes her hair after her shower.

Henry watches the television his family brought from home.

Estella and Jorge preparing fajitas.

Children pick cucumbers in the midday sun.

"*There were no trees. In the Panhandle, with 100 degrees, you had to find shade somewhere. Sometimes we didn't.*"

Rafael Guerra
Educator and former migrant worker

"*It was especially hard during the hottest parts of the day. The sand would be so hot that it shined. You could see the wavey reflection as if it were water.*"

Hector J. Cruz
Former migrant worker

Gabriel Lopes and brother Ramondo Jr. resting under truck in cucumber field.

"Families work around pesticides. They don't know it. Farmers spray on weekends, families start working again Monday. Kids develop rashes, red eyes, sore throat—blame it on the heat. Upset stomach also. High rate of cancer, and kidney problems. Often by 45 they're on dialysis."

Trini Gomez
Panhandle social worker and former migrant worker

"I don't know what the kids are doing here. They're just here. It's not so bad today in there."

Panhandle grower spraying herbicide as child hoes cotton

"And we would work Saturday and Sunday also. We wouldn't have a day off, until one day we all requested one day off. So we could go dancing. To go dancing in Bakersfield."

Maria Victoria Cruz
Former migrant worker

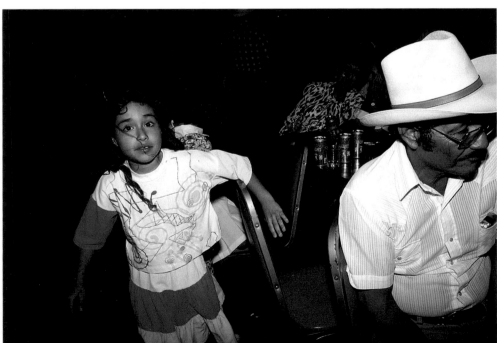

Saturday night dance in Plainview.

"Farmwork is very difficult. I want my kids to study to do better. We bring them to the fields to see how difficult the work is. Not even the oldest, in tenth grade, wants to work in the fields."

Flor Cervantes (mother)
Homestead, Florida

Adriana Cervantes, 8, and her brother, George, 13, weeding tomato fields.

"*You are treated like an adult and you're expected to act like an adult when you're in the field. Then you hit the schools and all of a sudden you are a child and you are just a ten year old, you are a kid.*"

Rafael Guerra
Educator and former migrant worker

Flora Cervantes, 6, and her family.

"We go to the fields and weed and pick. It's hard because we don't eat until we get home. Sometimes I like for school vacation to be over so we don't have to go to the fields."

Luisa Cervantes, age 11

Flor Cervantes, weeding tomatoes.

Adriana, Flor and a younger brother at a labor camp in South Dade.

Adriana and her brother inside the camp.

String bean field.

Father and son at labor camp.

Farmworker children at the Redlands Christian Migrant
Association day care center in the South Dade labor camp.

String bean fields.

"*I worked hard to stop migrating to help my children. When you're traveling around it's always a problem to put the kids in school or find babysitting.*"

Petra Gonzalez
South Dade outreach worker and former migrant worker

South Dade labor camp.

Viravon Keophila, 6, and sister Uppakorn, 8, Laotian children harvesting herbs.

"We were always very happy. We were never forced to be out there. We were out there because we wanted to help Mom and Dad. And that's how life was."

Hector J. Cruz
Former migrant worker

Uppakorn holding tarpaulin as mother, Malaky, trims herbs.

Keophila sisters playing on truck.

The family picks herbs.

"Farmwork is not a pretty sight. It's very difficult. You have to keep working even if it is raining, or whatever the weather is, just because the "patron" wants you to. When you migrate you don't know where you are going to live, in a dirty hotel or labor camp with many other people. If the job isn't good, sometimes you don't even have enough money to return. Some places don't have day care and you don't know what to do with your kids then. You have to put up with a lot and endure. It's uncomfortable to get rid of your things every three months and get new things when you get to the next place. My kids are in school now and don't have too many absences. They get to finish a whole year at one school, so they don't have as many problems passing. I want them to have good careers and progress."

Francisco Loredo
South Dade outreach worker and former migrant worker

Viravon on top of the family truck.

"You know, people, they sit down and have a great salad and they don't know where it comes from. They think it comes from H.E.B. or Foy's or somewhere like that. Somebody has to pick that asparagus, somebody has to pick all the fruits and vegetables. It's estimated that every farmer feeds approximately 75 people in the world."

Román Cruz
Outreach worker and former migrant worker

Asparagus harvest, Sunnyside.

"Many people say, ah, it's unskilled labor. It's not unskilled labor, you have to know how to cut the asparagus, you have to know which size to pick it, you have to know which size to clip it and not pick it."

Román Cruz
Outreach worker and former migrant worker

Myrna Garcia, 18, cutting asparagus.

Myrta Garcia, 4, and sister, Maria, 9, wait in truck while older sisters work in the fields.

Minerva Garcia, 16, checks on her younger sisters.

"We start picking asparagus as soon as it gets light. We use the light from the cars. If it's really hot you can't stay too late, you get more tired and everything like that. This year the latest we picked was about one o'clock." Minerva Garcia, 16

Growers eat breakfast at flapjack house in Sunnyside.

Eric Mendiola, 8, harvesting asparagus with his family, Pasco.

Migrant children at Quonset-style World War II barracks, Eltopia.

"And during the days that we did laundry we would sleep about 3 hours total. There were times that we had over $2,000 in checks and we couldn't buy groceries because we didn't have time to go to the bank to cash the checks."

Valente Elizondo
Migrant worker

Extended migrant family made up of the Abundiz, Cortez, Solis and Gonzales families who live together in the former barracks.

Children at barracks camp.

Inside barracks: Cynthia Abundiz hugs grandmother.

Cortez family.

Yadira Cortez takes care of siblings.

Drying beef in the Abundiz kitchen inside barracks.

Teenage girl in her barracks bedroom.

Yadira Cortez.

"That little girl became a parent right there and then. The migrant child is going to babysit for four or five kids and feed them, they expect her to be there and take care of those kids. That's why by the time they're twelve or thirteen, if they know how to cook and everything, some of those kids are ready for marriage."

Rafael Guerra
Educator and former migrant worker

St. Joseph Catholic Church, Sunnyside. Special services are held in Spanish on Saturday night for the migrant families who will be working in the fields on Sunday. During the asparagus harvest not a day can be missed or the crop will perish.

82

Migrant families at Spring carnival in Sunnyside.

Migrant family leaving Washington State for the next harvest. Families move approximately every three months.

"What are some of the worries your parents have when you're on the road?"
"Probably stopping and fueling up and buying us food."
"Have they ever had problems finding a place to fuel up, to buy groceries?"
"Yes."
"What happens when that goes on?"
"Well, we keep on moving."

Santiago Olivarez III with father, Santiago Jr., washing his car, the family's most important possession.

"How long does it take you to go from here to Washington?"
"Two and a half days."
"And when you go from Washington to Illinois, how long does that take you?"
"Two days and a half."
"When you stop for eating or fueling up the truck, how are you treated in the different areas?"
"Well, they just look at you like weird. Like where are you coming from."

Santiago Olivarez III.

"I couldn't reach the conveyor belt, but I wanted to work. I would use the operator's tool box to stand on. Then I could reach the belt."

Former migrant worker

Araceli Ramerez, 8, and brother, Jose, 11, using a plastic water bottle to play tether ball.

Mabton labor camp.

"We're no second-class citizens. We are Americans. We're born and raised here in the United States, and our kids were born and raised here. Why are we being treated like this? We labor the fields, we bring the fruits to your table, and the sparkling wine, and yet you do not want to give us the right to go home and sleep on a Beauty Rest mattress."

Rafael Guerra
Educator and former migrant worker

"We'll rest for a while, then take a shower to get ready to go to school. The bus gets there at 4 and you have to be ready to go." She will be back in the fields by 5 the next morning.

Minerva Garcia

A career awareness assembly for migrant students at the Pasco night school.

Children returning by bus to the labor camps from the Washington State Migrant Council Head Start Center in Mabton.

93

Mabton Head Start

Nursery at the Eltopia Texas Migrant Council Head Start.

Migrant child at Mabton Head Start.

"Once California belonged to Mexico and its land to Mexicans; and a horde of tattered feverish Americans poured in. And such was their hunger for land that they took the land – stole Sutter's land, Guerrero's land, took the grants and broke them up and growled and quarreled over them, those frantic hungry men; and they guarded with guns the land they had stolen. They put up houses and barns, they turned the earth and planted crops. And these things were possession, and possession was ownership.

"The Mexicans were weak and fled. They could not resist because they wanted nothing in the world as frantically as the Americans wanted land."

John Steinbeck
"The Grapes of Wrath," 1939

"We speak very few words in English. We left our country to look for a better way of life. Here we do the labor in the fields. Here when there is work they call us. But sometimes they pay you when they get good and ready. Once I didn't get my check until four months later, because they think that we are not from this country. But I have my legalization papers. I can do a formal complaint. I don't do so because of different reasons, such as we don't have a car to move about from one office to another."

Mexican farmworker
Parlier, California, 1992

"I come from Arcelia, Guerrero. Many of the people have returned to Mexico without hope, they felt it was futile to stay here and just survive. Many of us are deciding to return to Mexico, whatever the pay may be."

Mexican farmworker
Del Mar, California, 1992

Southern California freeway.

Mexican family recently arrived in California and looking for work.

"From $3.25 down to $2.50 a box. About two boxes an hour. We come
during the season. We come and earn money, but we leave it here. They think -
come and take the money elsewhere, but not really. The food is very expensive.
rent is very expensive. Everything is expensive. Well, if you excuse me, I have t
load boxes."

Jose, an olive picker in Cor

Olive grove in Corning.

Brenda, 6, Ramon, 2, and Ye[...]
Corning during the harve[...]

"I seen pitchers of a country flat an' green, an' with little houses like Ma says, white. Ma got her heart set on a white house. Get to thinkin' they ain't no such country. I seen pitchers like that."
"Pa said, 'Wait till we get to California. You'll see nice country then."
"Jesus Christ, Pa! This here is California."

John Steinbeck
"The Grapes of Wrath," 1939

Migrant camp, Del Mar, early morning.

Jaime, 4, at the Del Mar camp, waiting for his sis

Jaime watches his father, who cannot find work, eat lunch.

Migrant ch

Joyita Mendez (month of flowers) after bath.

Father watching television, Del Mar camp.

Mother with children after bath, Del Mar camp.

Apolinar Macedo.

"They just come in once in a while to look at the place to make sure that it is being kept clean."

Faustino Macedo

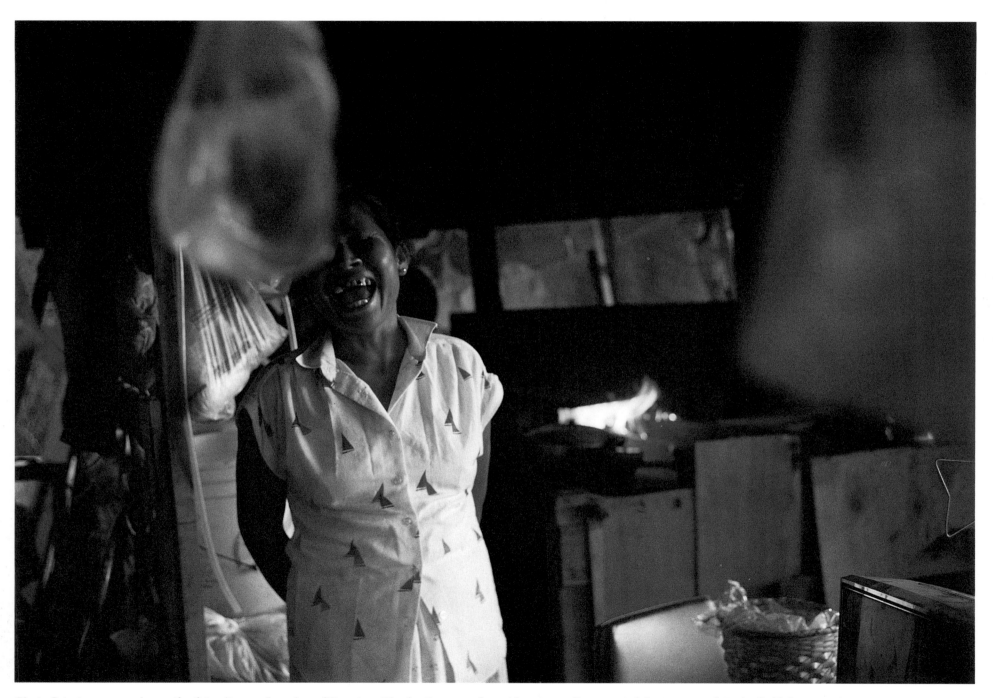

Gloria Crispin, common-law-wife of Apolinar and mother of Faustino. The family comes from Altamirano, Guerrero in Mexico to work in the Del Mar nurseries.

Noemi, 3, with mother, 19, in plywood shack.

Toilet facilities, Del Mar camp.

Bath.

Joyita Mendez with father working on truck.

Federico Cobos playing in the family truck.

Sofia Cruz and daughter, Michelle Rodriguez.

"In every child who is born, under no matter what circumstances, and of no matter what parents, the potentiality of the human race is born again: and in him, too, once more, and of each of us, our terrific responsibility towards human life…"

James Agee
"Let Us Now Praise Famous Men," 1939

"It wasn't just the work that was hard. Housing was almost nonexistent.
We had to leave big deposits in case the house was not left in a clean state. But everytime when we moved in, the housing we would get was in terrible shape and filthy. Grime on the floors and things, and the furniture was old and beaten.
It usually took us about a week to clean the place up. But it better be clean when we left otherwise we would not get our deposits back. That happened everywhere we went."

Valente Elizondo
Former migrant worker

A child playing in The Palacio (The Palace), the local name for these migrant quarters in Parlier, California.

Father and son in The Palacio.

Mother and daughter in The Palacio.

"Of course if you are pessimistic, it will be ugly. If you look at it from a positive side, you will take it like a game."

Sandra, 16-year-old living at The Palacio

Child resting at The Palacio.

Her brother hangs laundry outside a shack used for storage and sometimes sleeping.

Life at The Palacio.

Migrant boy and his pet rooster.

"There are more children here than adults." A father at The Palacio

Evening at The Palacio: Husbands to feed.

"Let me give you an idea of how it was. You're getting ready to go up North. The father would make a decision with his compadre. We are going to go to Plainview, we are going to go to California. But as soon as the decision was made, the mother was the one that started putting things together, whatever we were going to take up North.

"It was the mother that would cook the pinole or whatever she could take on the road. The mother was worried all the time. What do you do when you're in the truck and you're together with thirty or forty other people, and sometimes you don't even know the people. It was the mother who had to worry all day—I hope my son won't have diarrhea. And if he has diarrhea, how do you take care of it in the truck when the truck is driving and the crew leader is not going to stop.

"And then we got to the place. It was the mother who was hoping for the best living area, which was not much, maybe a 12-by-12 little shack or together with everybody else. Sometimes they'd put three or four families in one long barrack, but she had to find a little corner where she was going to put her stove which was made out of kerosene.

"But comes day to work, the mother would get up an hour before anybody else. She was the one who had to get the food ready. Cook the breakfast okay. Cook the breakfast early, so you could see that little burner, and you could see that kerosene, and you were under the covers because it was cold and you were hoping it wasn't time to get up. But it was time."

Rafael Guerra

Volleyball game among migrants in Parlier.

Migrant child attending elementary school in San Luis Obispo.

"One of the hardest things was having to go to school up there with the Anglos. They'd make fun of us. They'd call us names and yell at us Mexicans. I'd feel out of place. I didn't like that."

Hector J. Cruz
Former migrant worker

Two-year-old boy helping father pick olives in Corning.

"I think of the migrant child as a handicapped child. He's somebody else's problem. They let him go from place to place and then he moves down the road and becomes somebody else's problem. Out of sight out of mind."

Rafael Guerra
Migrant educator and former migrant worker

AFTERWORD

by Rubén Blades

In America, life can sometimes feel like a death sentence.

Living can hurt. It can cost immensely.

No one pays a higher price than children.

No one consults them; they have absolutely no say in adults' decisions.

They can't choose families, or the environment in which to nurture their young hope.

Children are more than witnesses; they are protagonists. The proof is in these pictures by Nancy Buirski. Whether it's a Laotian girl in Homestead, Florida, or Susy Zavala, age 12, cotton hoer in Plainview, Texas, their wonderland is one of sacrifices and hardships.

In America, increasingly so, children are born to later become crushed or lost beneath the "tomorrows" their parents live and die for.

A family's effort is but one single struggle, one collective sweat, one unified purpose.

America is one big house of hopes, young and old. But children seem always to end up with the short end of the stick.

Let us respect their innocence, so that we may preserve whatever is left of ours. Let us give them our attention whenever possible, so that we may tend to the best of emotions: unselfishness.

Let us protect our children, help them to grow up, not down.

Maybe one day, we'll see a picture of an America where living doesn't hurt anyone, where we perpetuate a cycle of love and compassion that cannot, ever, be broken.

Rubén Blades, October 27, 1993